Garfield
swallows his pride

BY: JIM DAVIS

BALLANTINE BOOKS · NEW YORK

10

WOULDN'T YOU KNOW IT? THERE'S A CAT HAIR IN MY LASAGNA

5-9

© 1986 United Feature Syndicate, Inc.

WHAT DO YOU HAVE TO SAY FOR YOURSELF?

OUCH!

JIM DAVIS

5-10

© 1986 United Feature Syndicate, Inc.

CRASH!

WHAT MADE YOU DO THAT?

MY SENSE OF AESTHETICS

JIM DAVIS

YOU KNOW, BOYS, IT'S NICE TO SPEND SOME QUALITY TIME TOGETHER AND REALLY VISIT

REMEMBER THE TIME YOU GOT WRAPPED UP IN THE WINDOW BLIND, GARFIELD?

© 1986 United Feature Syndicate, Inc.

AND THEN I GOT CAUGHT IN IT TRYING TO GET YOU FREE?

THEN, TO TOP IT OFF, ODIE GOT CAUGHT IN IT TRYING TO SAVE US!

IT SEEMS LIKE ONLY YESTERDAY

5-18

IT WAS YESTERDAY, YOU TWIT!

URF

NO YOU CAN'T GO OUT, ODIE!

JIM DAVIS

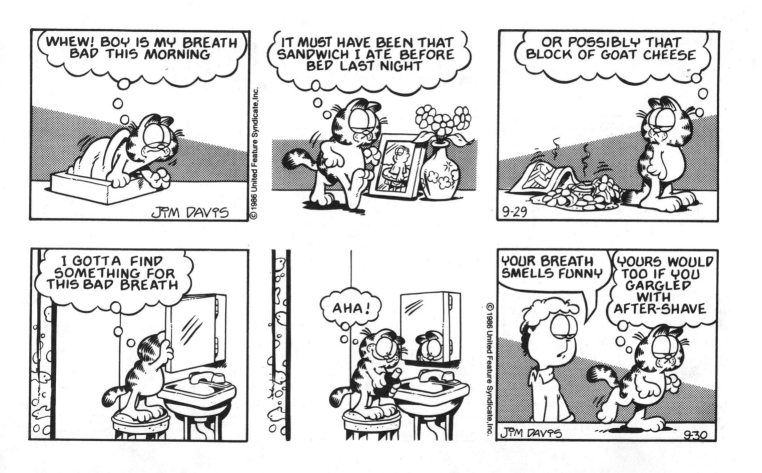

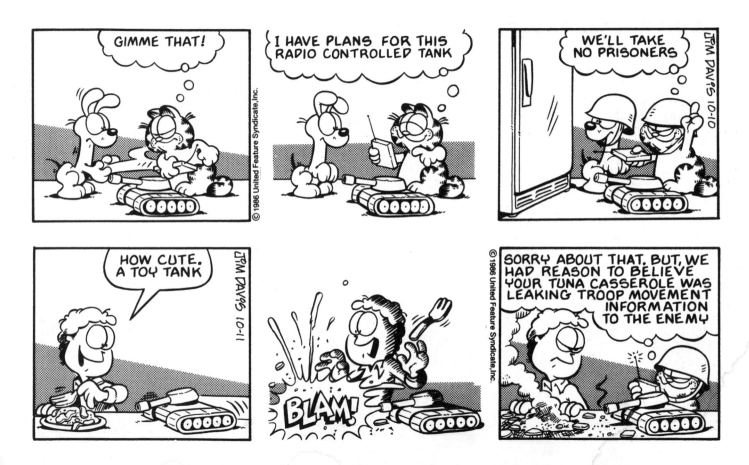

STRIPS, SPECIALS OR BESTSELLING BOOKS . . .
GARFIELD'S ON EVERYONE'S MENU
Don't miss even one episode in the Tubby Tabby's hilarious series!

__GARFIELD AT LARGE (#1)   32013/$6.95
__GARFIELD GAINS WEIGHT (#2)   32008/$6.95
__GARFIELD BIGGER THAN LIFE (#3)   32007/$6.95
__GARFIELD WEIGHS IN (#4)   32010/$6.95
__GARFIELD TAKES THE CAKE (#5)   32009/$6.95
__GARFIELD EATS HIS HEART OUT (#6)   32018/$6.95
__GARFIELD SITS AROUND THE HOUSE (#7)   32011/$6.95
__GARFIELD TIPS THE SCALES (#8)   33580/$6.95
__GARFIELD LOSES HIS FEET (#9)   31805/$6.95
__GARFIELD MAKES IT BIG (#10)   31928/$6.95
__GARFIELD ROLLS ON (#11)   32634/$6.95
__GARFIELD OUT TO LUNCH (#12)   33118/$6.95
__GARFIELD FOOD FOR THOUGHT (#13)   34129/$6.95

__GARFIELD SWALLOWS HIS PRIDE (#14)   34725/$6.95
__GARFIELD WORLDWIDE (#15)   35158/$6.95
__GARFIELD ROUNDS OUT (#16)   35388/$6.95
__GARFIELD CHEWS THE FAT (#17)   35956/$6.95
__GARFIELD GOES TO WAIST (#18)   36430/$6.95
__GARFIELD HANGS OUT (#19)   36835/$6.95
__GARFIELD TAKES UP SPACE (#20)   37029/$6.95
__GARFIELD SAYS A MOUTHFUL (#21)   37368/$6.95
__GARFIELD BY THE POUND (#22)   37579/$6.95
__GARFIELD KEEPS HIS CHINS UP (#23)   37959/$6.95
__GARFIELD TAKES HIS LICKS (#24)   38170/$6.95
__GARFIELD HITS THE BIG TIME (#25)   38332/$6.95

GARFIELD AT HIS SUNDAY BEST!
__GARFIELD TREASURY   32106/$9.95
__THE SECOND GARFIELD TREASURY   33276/$10.95
__THE THIRD GARFIELD TREASURY   32635/$11.00
__THE FOURTH GARFIELD TREASURY   34726/$10.95
__THE FIFTH GARFIELD TREASURY   36268/$12.00
__THE SIXTH GARFIELD TREASURY   37367/$10.95

Please send me the BALLANTINE BOOKS I have checked above. I am
enclosing $_____. (Please add $2.00 for the first book and $.50
for each additional book for postage and handling and include the appropriate
state sales tax.) Send check or money order (no cash or C.O.D.'s) to
Ballantine Mail Sales Dept. TA, 400 Hahn Road, Westminster, MD 21157.

To order by phone, call 1-800-733-3000 and use your major credit card.

Prices and numbers are subject to change without notice. Valid in the U.S.
only. All orders are subject to availability.

Name_____

Address_____

City_____ State_____ Zip_____

Allow at least 4 weeks for delivery   7/93